"The eye-searing smoke; the crackle and roar of flame devouring dead wood and live trees, whipped up by sudden, powerful and sustained gusts of wind; a whole hillside clear and green in the morning, burning brightly by nightfall; Old Faithful erupting at the height of the tourist season — but without another soul in sight: these are the vivid and unforgettable memories of my first visit to Yellowstone in the momentous summer of 1988. I was there during the worst of the firestorms. Like many of the tourists, I offered my assistance — but the firefighters needed experienced helpers.

"Here, then, is the story of those firefighters' heroic and exhausting battles. And more: here is the dramatic story of a wild and beautiful park in transition, and revelation of the surprising and vital role that fire plays in the natural cycle of the wilderness."

Gareth Stevens

Gareth Stevens, Publisher

The photographs in this book were previously used in an adult book titled *Yellowstone on Fire*, published by the Billings Gazette of Billings, Montana. The Billings Gazette is the largest newspaper in Montana, and its extensive coverage of the Yellowstone fires later became a finalist in the 1989 Pulitzer Prize competition.
See page 32 for details.

FIRE!
IN YELLOWSTONE
A TRUE ADVENTURE

Library of Congress Cataloging-in-Publication Data

Ekey, Robert.
    Fire! in Yellowstone.
    (True adventures)

    Summary: Discusses the fire that ravaged nearly one million
acres of Yellowstone National Park during several months in
1988, and explains the two sides to the controversy over
letting nature take its course.
    1. Forest fires—Yellowstone National Park—Juvenile
literature. 2. Forest fires—Government policy—Yellowstone National Park—Juvenile literature. 3. Yellowstone
National Park—Juvenile literature. 4. Fire ecology—
Yellowstone National Park—Juvenile literature. [1. Forest
fires—Yellowstone National Park. 2. Yellowstone National
Park. 3. Fire ecology. 4. Ecology] I. Title. II. Series.
SD421.32.Y45E379   1989
634.9'618'0978752   89-43156
ISBN 0-8368-0226-8

ISBN Gareth Stevens 0-8368-0226-8 (lib. bdg.)
ISBN Gareth Stevens 0-8368-0259-4 (softcover)
ISBN Falcon Press 0-937959-93-6 (hardcover)

This edition first published in 1990 by
Gareth Stevens, Inc., in association with Falcon Press, Inc.

Text copyright © 1990 by Falcon Press Publishing Co., Inc.
Photographs from *Yellowstone on Fire* copyright © 1989 by
The Billings Gazette. Additional photos copyright © 1990 by
Bob Zellar and Larry Mayer. Format copyright © 1990 by
Gareth Stevens, Inc.

Designer: Kate Kriege
Editor: Rhoda Irene Sherwood

Printed in the United States of America

1 2 3 4 5 6 7 8 9 96 95 94 93 92 91 90

Picture Credits
Robert Ekey: 20-21; Larry Mayer: 4, 7, 8-9, 10, 12 (upper inset), 12-13, 14,
15, 16, 17, 18 (insets), 22-23, 25, 26 (left inset), 26-27 (background), 28, 29;
Judy Tell: 20 (inset); James Woodcock: 24; Bob Zellar: cover, 5, 6, 11, 12
(lower inset), 18-19, 26 (right inset), 27 (inset). Illustrations originally
published by The Billings Gazette in the book *Yellowstone on Fire*; artwork
by John Potter: 30, 31.

FIRE!
IN YELLOWSTONE
A TRUE ADVENTURE

Story by Robert Ekey

Gareth Stevens Children's Books
MILWAUKEE

In 1988, spring came early in Yellowstone National Park. Snow that usually stays until June melted away under bright, sunny skies. Little rain fell.

The elk, moose, and grizzly bears grazed on an abundant supply of grass and other plants. Old Faithful geyser gushed as tourists snapped photographs. Yellowstone did not appear to be in a drought, but the forest was dry.

Far left: Elk graze, undisturbed by the antics of the geysers. Even during the fire, most animals were calm despite the raging fires and the activities of the firefighters and soldiers.

Upper left: A bear and cub near Mystic Falls. Most animals escaped the dangerous fires.

In June, a bolt of lightning struck a tree and started a small forest fire. Soon, lightning struck in other areas and started more fires in Yellowstone and on nearby forest lands. Each fire sent up a small column of smoke.

At first, park rangers allowed the fires to burn. Rangers had learned that fire has always been a vital part of the forest ecology, or the relationship between living things and their surroundings. Fire clears away old trees to make room for new plants and trees. Fires are as important to the growth of the forest as sunshine and rain.

Far left: Fire creeps up the dry trunks of trees near Grant Village in Yellowstone.

Left: Fishing in the Firehole River. At first, people went about doing their normal activities.

7

This was not the first time
Yellowstone had seen fires.
Every year lightning starts fires.
In fact, centuries ago, Native
Americans used to light fires
to drive game to hunters and to
improve wildlife habitats.

Most of the fires that start go out
by themselves. Those that burn
usually burn only a few acres.
But 1988 was a different year.
The heat of the summer and lack
of rain left the forest very dry.

The fires in and near Yellowstone
grew bigger. A careless woodcutter
started another fire.

The North Fork fire south of the town called West
Yellowstone. This damaging fire was accidentally
started by a woodcutter in Idaho's Targhee National
Forest, only 200 yards from Yellowstone.

By the end of July, fires were close to buildings, and tourists moved from their campsites. Rangers decided they should try to put out all fires.

Most states sent firefighters to Yellowstone to battle the blazes. These young men and women fought hard to control the fires.

Far left: Near Norris, where the historic log museum stands. Fires closed roads, so tourists moved to the safe sections of the park.

Far left, inset: Taking a rest after clearing trails. As tourists were asked to leave, firefighters set up their camps in tourist campgrounds.

Left: Red fire, near Lewis Lake, which is in southern Yellowstone. Firefighter Jill Jayne studies the fire as it moves through the treetops.

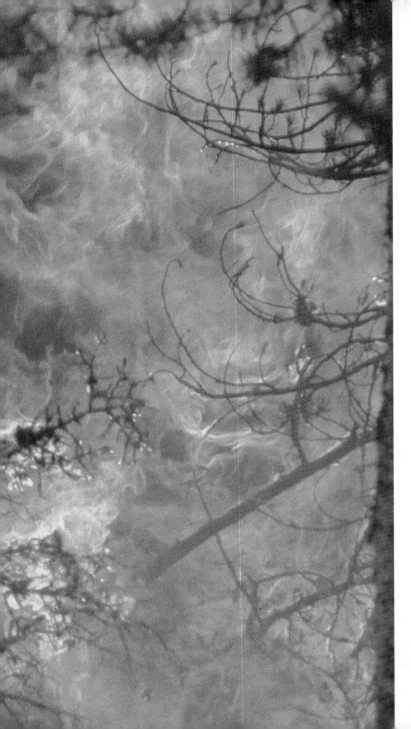

But by August, the fires had continued to spread. No rain fell, and winds fanned the flames. Some days, the wind blew at gale force, spreading the fires over thousands of acres. Flames 200 feet tall swept through the forest faster than people can walk.

As the fires burned in the forest, the elk, bison, and other animals could easily escape the flames. Sometimes they were seen calmly grazing near the fires.

Left, upper inset: Bison calm in the midst of fires. Elk and moose often entered burned areas to eat. They wanted the minerals which were contained in the ashes.

Left, lower inset: Clover-Mist fire at the foot of Pilot Peak. A dangerous fire but beautiful at night.

Background: In late July, gale-force winds fan a fire near Grant Village.

Many people who live near Yellowstone asked why rangers did not put out the fires. By then, the fires were too big. The worst drought in a century had left the forest too dry. The fires could not be stopped.

Thousands of firefighters were called to help, including soldiers from the U.S. Army and Marines. They used helicopters and airplanes to drop millions of gallons of water and chemicals on the fires. Firefighters used special tools to dig trails in the forest, in an attempt to stop the flames.

Firefighting, modern and traditional: Firefighters used planes to take infrared maps of the land. They flew air tankers carrying water and chemicals that retard flames. They called in fire trucks from many stations. But to do this grueling work, they also had to use shovels, mules, and Pulaskis (a combination hoe and axe).

Every morning, smoke blanketed Yellowstone. Every afternoon, high winds blew, sending burning embers flying high in the sky. When the embers landed, they started more fires. Thousands of acres were on fire, and huge smoke columns filled the sky.

Far left: Along the Gibbon River. The wind whipped these hundreds of small fires into a firestorm by morning.

Left: A smoke column rises near West Yellowstone. Fire feeds on oxygen and then blows it into the air as smoke.

17

In early September — when the smoke column showed the fire was moving closer — tourists were still visiting Old Faithful. Firefighters sprayed buildings with water to keep them from burning.

Suddenly, the fire crested the ridge near Old Faithful! Rangers ordered tourists to leave quickly. A fierce firestorm swept across the parking lot near the old hotel there. It sent embers the size of golf balls skipping across the pavement.

Far left inset: Wetting the roof of the Norris Museum to protect it from embers.

Right inset: When fires closed roads, employees of the park helped tourists find safe routes out.

Background: A smoke cloud hovers over Old Faithful. Just hours later, a firestorm would sweep through this area.

The firestorm surprised firefighters. Many raced to help protect buildings and put out small fires started by the embers.

The fire at Old Faithful burned many trees and a few small cabins. But the larger buildings were saved, including the big old log hotel called the Old Faithful Inn. The fire seemed to pass as quickly as it came.

Inset: Spraying the roof of the Old Faithful Inn. That morning, there had been nearly 700 guests at the inn. But park officials had to ask them to leave.

Background: The North Fork fire consumes one of the buildings of the Old Faithful complex. Flames devoured 16 buildings in all.

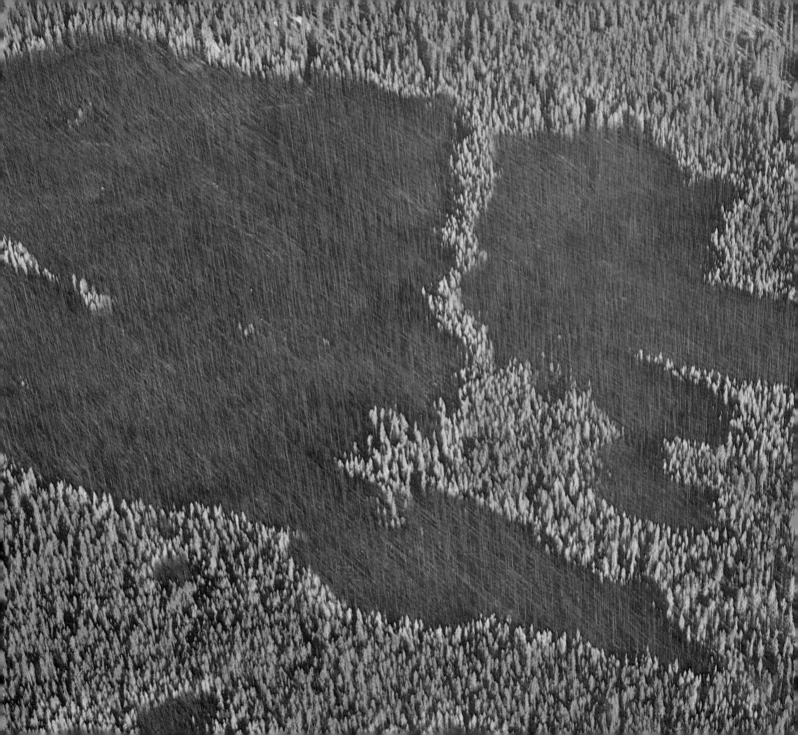

The next week, it started to rain and snow. It was the first rain in the park in weeks. The rain did what ten thousand firefighters could not do — it started to put the fires out.

By mid-September, nearly one million acres had burned in Yellowstone and 400 thousand in nearby forests. The area burned is the same size as the state of Delaware, but still less than half of the park was burned.

Background: A pattern of burned forest in the North Fork area. The mix of burned areas and green vegetation shows that the fires did not consume everything in their path.

Inset: Snows in September sent military firefighters to the camp stove to warm up.

During the fires, many people argued that Yellowstone officials should have tried to put the fires out sooner. The officials answered that they could not have forecast the extreme drought conditions.

Only nature could stop what it started with the drought. "This is Mother Nature at work," one park ranger said. In the future, rangers decided, some fires will still be allowed to burn, but they will be watched more closely.

Far left: Firefighter Mark Courson directs other firefighters along a bulldozed fire line. Park officials did not want to bulldoze lines, for these lines scar the land more than fires do. But they finally decided to bulldoze in an attempt to stop the fires.

Left: People who live in Cooke City, just outside Yellowstone, ask a National Park Service employee if their homes are in danger.

Snow covered Yellowstone early in October. Early the next spring, the snow melted, providing water for the seeds and roots that had survived underground.

Where meadows had been burned, wildflowers bloomed in the spring and summer. In the forested areas, thousands of lodgepole pine seedlings sprouted as the forest was born again. None of the geysers was changed by the fire.

Background: The ash from blackened growth is filled with minerals. Carried by rain into the soil, it makes the forest land richer.

Left inset: Grass sprouts from the charred earth near Grant Village.

Middle inset: By spring, flowers are blooming and spreading through the forest.

Right inset: The heat of the fire caused lodgepole pine seeds to pop from their cones. They then rooted in the fertile ash and are now becoming a new forest.

While fire forced some animals to move from the forest, it also provided new food sources for other wildlife. Biologists say that animals and plants adapt to fire. For some animals, fire even makes life easier.

Now, much rain has fallen, and the drought is over. Elk and bison graze on the new wildflowers and grasses. Birds sing in the trees. And tourists return to take pictures of the animals, the geysers, and the fresh young plants growing from the forest floor.

Tourists once again flock to Yellowstone, where they see that plants grew back more quickly in some areas of the park than in others. Regrowth occurs more quickly in areas where there is moisture and where the heat from the fire was not too intense. Intense heat destroys plant roots.

Where is Yellowstone?

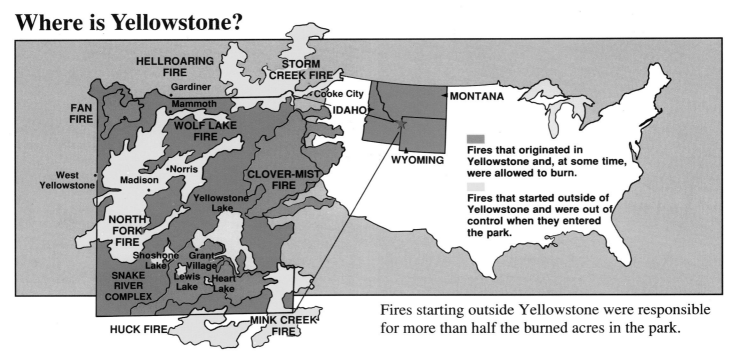

HELLROARING FIRE

STORM CREEK FIRE

Gardiner

Cooke City

Mammoth

IDAHO

MONTANA

FAN FIRE

WOLF LAKE FIRE

Norris

West Yellowstone

Madison

CLOVER-MIST FIRE

WYOMING

Yellowstone Lake

NORTH FORK FIRE

Shoshone Lake

Grant Village

Lewis Lake

Heart Lake

SNAKE RIVER COMPLEX

HUCK FIRE

MINK CREEK FIRE

■ Fires that originated in Yellowstone and, at some time, were allowed to burn.

■ Fires that started outside of Yellowstone and were out of control when they entered the park.

Fires starting outside Yellowstone were responsible for more than half the burned acres in the park.

To Learn More About Forest Fires, Conservation of Our Forests, and Other Concerns About the Environment . . .

Organizations

The events narrated in this book are true. Many people in and around Yellowstone offered their help in attempting to control the devastating fires of 1988. To learn more about Yellowstone National Park, forests, and wildlife, write to the following addresses and be sure to include your name, address, and age.

Greater Yellowstone Coalition
P.O. Box 1874
Bozeman, MT 59715

National Parks and Conservation Association
1015 31st Street NW
Washington, DC 20007

National Wildlife Federation
1412 16th Street NW
Washington, DC 20036

Sierra Club
730 Polk Street
San Francisco, CA 94109

The Wilderness Society
1400 Eye Street NW
Washington, DC 20005

World Wildlife Fund
1250 24th Street NW
Washington, DC 20037

Yellowstone Institute
P.O. Box 1117
Yellowstone National Park, WY 82190

Yellowstone National Park
Office of Interpretation
P.O. Box 168
Yellowstone National Park, WY 82190

Books

The books listed below will tell you more about forest fires and about other issues pertaining to our natural environment. Check your local library or bookstore to see if they have them or can order them for you.

Expedition Yellowstone: A Mountain Adventure.
   Robinson (Rinehart, Roberts)
One Day in the Alpine Tundra.
   George (Harper & Row Junior)

Yellowstone National Park. Radlauer (Childrens Press)
Yellowstone on Fire (The Billings Gazette) (See p. 32)
Young People's Guide to Yellowstone Park.
   Tawney (Stoneydale Press)

Illustration of a lodgepole forest, showing a life cycle of 250 to 400 years.

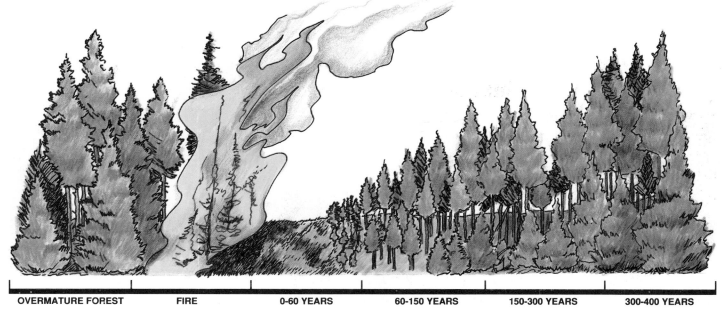

| OVERMATURE FOREST | FIRE | 0-60 YEARS | 60-150 YEARS | 150-300 YEARS | 300-400 YEARS |

A List of Words About Forests, Fires, and Firefighting

Listed below are some words used in this book. You can read what they mean, see them used in a sentence, and turn to the pages listed after each definition to see where they appeared in this book.

acre — a measure of land that is 43,560 square feet. There are 640 acres in a square mile.   13, 17, 23
At 57,600 square feet, a U.S. football field is larger than an acre.

biologist — a person who studies animal and plant life.   29
A biologist can tell you many interesting facts about the way the human body works.

bison — the American buffalo, a beast with four legs, a shaggy mane, and a humped back.   13, 29
A bison looks a bit like an ox, but with a furry collar and beard.

drought — a prolonged period of dry weather.   5, 15, 25, 29
A place that often suffers from drought is called a dust bowl.

ecology — the study of the relationships between plants, animals, and other living things and their environment.   7
Some colleges now have programs in which students specialize in ecology.

elk — a large deer that has some features of a moose.   5, 29
The elk live in northern regions.

embers — glowing pieces of coal or wood.   17, 19, 21
When a fire is dying out, the embers still provide warmth.

firestorm — an intense fire over a large area.   19
The animals fled as the firestorm approached.

gale — a wind with a speed of 32 to 63 miles per hour.   13
When a gale blows in from the sea, it often carries lots of water.

geyser — a spring that sends columns of boiling water and steam into the air at certain times.   5, 27, 29
Sometimes oil erupts from the ground in geysers.

habitat — the area where a plant or animal grows or lives naturally, where we are likely to find it.   9
Tadpoles, which become frogs, live in a watery habitat when young but move to a land habitat when they become adults.

infrared — a kind of radiation with longer wavelengths than the wavelengths of visible light; photographers use infrared devices to take pictures when there is no visible light.   15
Infrared pictures have helped pilots fly at night.

lodgepole pine — a type of pine tree that grows tall and thin in forests in the Rocky Mountains.   27
The lodgepole pine, from western North America, is often used in construction.

A lodgepole pine cone with seeds, after the fire.

Fire! in Yellowstone is adapted from an adult book, *Yellowstone on Fire*, which contains 100 outstanding color photographs of the historic forest fires and heroic firefighting efforts in addition to a comprehensive text. The 128-page, 8 1/2" x 11" book retails for $12.95 plus $1.50 for postage and handling. For copies of *Yellowstone on Fire*, write The Billings Gazette, P.O. Box 36300, Billings, MT 59601 or call (406) 657-1200.